PLAY
SUDOKU

LEARN FRENCH!

Berlitz Publishing
New York   Munich   Singapore

Play Sudoku Learn French!

No part of this book may be reproduced, stored in a retrieval system or transmitted in any form or means electronic, mechanical, photocopying, recording or otherwise, without prior written permission from APA Publications.

Contacting the Editors

Every effort has been made to provide accurate information in this publication, but changes are inevitable. The publisher cannot be responsible for any resulting loss, inconvenience or injury.
We would appreciate it if readers would call our attention to any errors or outdated information by contacting us at:
Email: comments@berlitzpublishing.com

Translation, adaptation and interior layout: Lingua Tech (S) Pte Ltd
Cover design concept: Leighanne Tillman
Cover layout: Lingua Tech (S) Pte Ltd
Cover illustrations: © Annsunnyday; Archana Bhartia; Parkbenchpics; Oleg Iatsun/Dreamstime.com

Contents

User's Guide — 05

Level 1: Eating

Meals Les repas	06
To eat and drink Manger et boire	06
On the table Sur la table	07
Condiments Les condiments	07
Where to buy things Où faire les commissions	08
Where to eat Où manger	08
Breakfast Le petit déjeuner	09
Nuts Les fruits secs	10
Vegetables Les légumes	10
Meat La viande	11
Seafood Les produits de la mer	11
Food Les aliments	12
Dessert Les desserts	12
Drinks Les boissons	13

Level 1: Vacations

Trips Les voyages	14
Destinations Les destinations	14
The hotel L'hôtel	15
Luggage Les bagages	15
Car La voiture	16
Plane L'avion	16
The farm La ferme	17
Rain La pluie	17
Family La famille	18
The playground L'aire de jeu	18
Playing Jouer	19
Swimming Nager	19
Travel Le voyage	20
The beach La plage	20
Family and friends Famille et amis	21
The farm La ferme	21

Contents

Level 2: Eating

On the table   Sur la table   22
At the restaurant   Au restaurant   23
Vegetables   Les légumes   24
Meat   La viande   25
Dishes   Les plats   26
Sandwich   Sandwich   27
Fruit   Les fruits   28
Amount   Quantités   29

Level 2: Vacations

City   La ville   30
Travel   Le voyage   31
The beach   La plage   32
The tour   La visite   34
The farm   La ferme   35
Amusement park   Le parc d'attractions   36
Camping   Le camping   37

Level 3: Eating

At the restaurant   Au restaurant   38
Taste   Les goûts   39
Meat and fish   Viande et poisson   40
Dishes   Les plats   41
Fruit   Les fruits   42
Vegetables   Les légumes   43
Cooking   Cuisiner   44
Party food   Les amuse-gueules   45

Level 3: Vacations

The beach   La plage   46
Winter   L'hiver   47
In the mountains   À la montagne   48
Travel   Le voyage   49
City   La ville   50
Postcards   Le courrier   51
Summer   L'été   52
Clothing   Les vêtements   53

Solutions and Index

Solutions   55
Index   71

Play Sudoku Learn French!

In this book, you will find over 60 puzzles or word games to help you learn French. Each puzzle provides a bite-sized vocabulary lesson that you can complete in minutes. Use your time on the bus, the train, or even the plane to expand your French vocabulary!

The book is divided into sections: Level 1, Level 2 and Level 3.
Each Level 1 puzzle consists of 16 cells in four '2 by 2' boxes in a '4 by 4' grid.
Each Level 2 puzzle consists of 36 cells in six '3 by 2' boxes in a '6 by 6' grid.
Each Level 3 puzzle consists of 81 cells in nine '3 by 3' boxes in a '9 by 9' grid.

The puzzles are organised by themes (which are listed in the Contents pages). Use the themes to direct you to specific topics (like 'Trips' and 'Travel') so that you can use the vocabulary right away.

How to play
Each puzzle comes with a short word list in French and English.
Fill each Sudoku cell with one word from the list while observing these rules:
• A word can only appear once in a row (across the grid).
• A word can only appear once in a column (down the grid).
• A word can only appear once in each box (marked with a bold border).
Refer to the Solutions pages at the back of the book for answers to all the puzzles.

Masculine and feminine forms

* Page 21: 'friend'; *ami* (masculine), *amie* (feminine)
'buddy'; *copain* (masculine), *copine* (feminine)

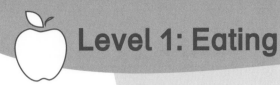

Level 1: Eating

Meals Les repas

dîner	déjeuner	casse-croûte	
	petit déjeuner		
		déjeuner	
		petit déjeuner	casse-croûte

breakfast	**petit déjeuner**
lunch	**déjeuner**
dinner	**dîner**
snack	**casse-croûte**

To eat and drink Manger et boire

	aliments	boire	
manger			aliments
boire			boisson
	boisson	manger	

to eat	**manger**
food	**aliments**
to drink	**boire**
beverage	**boisson**

On the table **Sur la table**

fourchette			cuiller
	serviette	couteau	
	cuiller	fourchette	
serviette			couteau

fork   **fourchette**
knife   **couteau**
spoon   **cuiller**
napkin   **serviette**

Condiments **Les condiments**

		huile d'olive	vinaigre
		poivre	sel
sel	poivre		huile d'olive
vinaigre	huile d'olive		

salt   **sel**
pepper   **poivre**
vinegar   **vinaigre**
olive oil   **huile d'olive**

Where to buy things Où faire les commissions

supérette	drugstore		
		drugstore	supérette
super-marché	centre commer-cial		
		centre commer-cial	super-marché

convenience store	**supérette**
drugstore	**drugstore**
supermarket	**super-marché**
mall	**centre commercia**

Where to eat   Où mange

		restaurant	café
restaurant	café		
snack-bar	pub		
		snack-bar	pub

restaurant	**restaurant**
café	**café**
snack bar	**snack-bar**
pub	**pub**

Breakfast Le petit déjeuner

			muffin
yaourt			céréales
			pain
céréales		muffin	

yogurt   **yaourt**
cereal   **céréales**
muffin   **muffin**
bread   **pain**

Breakfast Le petit déjeuner

		miel	beurre
miel			
	miel		fromage
confiture			

honey   **miel**
butter   **beurre**
cheese   **fromage**
jam   **confiture**

Nuts Les fruits secs

cacahuète			amande
	amande	noix de cajou	
amande	noix	cacahuète	noix de cajou

almond **amande**
walnut **noix**
peanut **cacahuète**
cashew nut **noix de cajou**

Vegetables Les légumes

			tomate
	carotte		
	tomate	ail	
oignon			

tomato **tomate**
carrot **carotte**
garlic **ail**
onion **oignon**

Meat **La viande**

viande	poulet		
			viande
poulet		porc	
	bœuf		poulet

meat	**viande**
chicken	**poulet**
beef	**bœuf**
pork	**porc**

Seafood **Les produits de la mer**

	crustacés	crevette	
poisson			calamar
crustacés			crevette
	poisson	calamar	

fish	**poisson**
shellfish	**crustacés**
shrimp	**crevette**
squid	**calamar**

Food Les aliments

	plat principal		salade
salade	soupe		
		hors-d'œuvre	soupe
soupe	hors-d'œuvre		

salad	**salade**
soup	**soupe**
appetiser	**hors-d'œuvre**
main course	**plat principal**

Dessert Les desserts

gâteau	fruit		
	glace		
	gelée	fruit	
		glace	gelée

cake	**gâteau**
ice cream	**glace**
jelly	**gelée**
fruit	**fruit**

Drinks **Les boissons**

jus de fruit			café
	lait	thé	
	jus de fruit	café	
lait			thé

juice	**jus de fruit**
milk	**lait**
tea	**thé**
coffee	**café**

Drinks **Les boissons**

	eau		
vin	boisson sans alcool	bière	eau
	bière	eau	
		boisson sans alcool	

water	**eau**
soft drink	**boisson sans alcool**
beer	**bière**
wine	**vin**

Level 1: Vacations

Trips **Les voyages**

hôtel	voyager	passeport	vacances
			voyager
passeport			
voyager	hôtel	vacances	passeport

vacation	**vacances**
hotel	**hôtel**
to travel	**voyager**
passport	**passeport**

Destinations **Les destination**

		ville	lac
ville	lac		
montagne	ville		
	plage	montagne	ville

beach	**plage**
city	**ville**
lake	**lac**
mountain	**montagne**

The hotel L'hôtel

chambre	réception	douche	
douche		chambre	
			douche
toilettes		réception	chambre

lobby	**réception**
room	**chambre**
shower	**douche**
toilet	**toilettes**

Luggage Les bagages

valise	bagages	sac à dos	bagage à main
bagages			sac à dos
	bagage à main	valise	

luggage	**bagages**
bag	**valise**
backpack	**sac à dos**
hand luggage	**bagage à main**

Car **La voiture**

	embou-teillage	ceinture de sécurité	
ceinture de sécurité			embou-teillage
conducteur			ceinture de sécurité
	ceinture de sécurité	conducteur	

to drive	**conduire**
driver	**conducteur**
seat belt	**ceinture de sécurité**
traffic jam	**embouteillage**

Plane **L'avion**

décoller			siège
	siège	décoller	
	embar-quement	siège	
siège			embar-quement

to take off	**décoller**
to land	**atterrir**
seat	**siège**
boarding	**embarquement**

16

The farm La ferme

cheval	vache	lapin	
		mouton	cheval
mouton			

horse	cheval
cow	vache
rabbit	lapin
sheep	mouton

Rain La pluie

pluie	imper-méable		blouson
	parapluie	blouson	pluie

rain	pluie
raincoat	imperméable
umbrella	parapluie
jacket	blouson

Family La famille

père			fille
		père	
fille			
mère			fils

father   **père**
mother   **mère**
son   **fils**
daughter **fille**

The playground L'aire de jeu

balançoire	bascule	toboggan	
		balançoire	bascule

ladder   **échelle**
seesaw   **bascule**
slide   **toboggan**
swing   **balançoire**

Playing **Jouer**

sauter	rire		
	courir		
		sauter	rire
		jouer	

to play **jouer**
to run **courir**
to jump **sauter**
to laugh **rire**

Swimming **Nager**

tongs	maillot de bain		
	tongs	slip de bain	bikini

bikini **bikini**
flip-flops **tongs**
swimsuit **maillot de bain**
trunks **slip de bain**

Travel Le voyage

	voiture		
	avion	autobus	
	autobus	bateau	
		voiture	

plane **avion**
bus **autobus**
car **voiture**
boat **bateau**

The beach La plage

sable		soleil	
soleil			
		vague	
vague		mer	

sun **soleil**
sand **sable**
sea **mer**
wave **vague**

Family and friends Famille et amis

colocataire	copain	famille	
	ami	copain	colocataire

*Refer to page 5 for masculine and feminine forms.

family	**famille**
friend	**ami***
buddy	**copain***
flatmate	**colocataire**

The farm La ferme

	tracteur		
	champ		
poney	champ	ferme	

farm	**ferme**
field	**champ**
pony	**poney**
tractor	**tracteur**

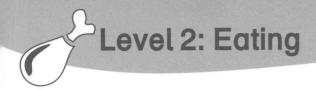
On the table Sur la table

		fourchette	cuiller	table	
table					couteau
	assiette	couteau		fourchette	
	verre			couteau	
couteau					table
		verre	couteau		

table	**table**	knife	**couteau**
plate	**assiette**	fork	**fourchette**
glass	**verre**	spoon	**cuiller**

At the restaurant **Au restaurant**

		servir	menu		
addition					serveur
	addition			commander	
	menu			serveuse	
serveuse					commander
		commander	serveuse		

waiter	**serveur**	to order	**commander**
waitress	**serveuse**	to serve	**servir**
menu	**menu**	bill	**addition**

Vegetables **Les légumes**

broccolis		chou-fleur	aubergine		
aubergine		chou			chou-fleur
navet		broccolis		chou	
potiron		aubergine	navet		
chou-fleur		navet		aubergine	
chou		potiron			navet

broccoli	**broccolis**	turnip	**navet**
cauliflower	**chou-fleur**	cabbage	**chou**
eggplant	**aubergine**	pumpkin	**potiron**

agneau		bacon		saucisse	
	hamburger		bifteck		bacon
	saucisse	hamburger	bacon		agneau
bacon		bifteck	saucisse	hamburger	
bifteck		agneau		dinde	
	dinde		agneau		bifteck

lamb	**agneau**	sausage	**saucisse**
bacon	**bacon**	steak	**bifteck**
hamburger	**hamburger**	turkey	**dinde**

Dishes Les plats

hot-dog	hamburger		omelette		soupe
tarte		soupe		spaghetti	
	soupe		tarte		omelette
hamburger		omelette		hot-dog	
	spaghetti		hot-dog		tarte
soupe		tarte		omelette	

hot dog	**hot-dog**
hamburger	**hamburger**
pie	**tarte**

soup	**soupe**
spaghetti	**spaghetti**
omelette	**omelette**

Sandwich Sandwich

ketchup	laitue	œuf			
fromage	jambon	tomate		ketchup	
tomate	œuf	laitue			
			œuf	laitue	tomate
	tomate		ketchup	œuf	jambon
			fromage	tomate	laitue

cheese	**fromage**	egg	**œuf**
lettuce	**laitue**	tomato	**tomate**
ham	**jambon**	ketchup	**ketchup**

Fruit Les fruits

				raisin	cerise	pomme
pomme	cerise	raisin				
				orange	citron	poire
citron	orange	poire				
poire	citron	cerise				
				citron	poire	cerise

apple	**pomme**		lemon	**citron**
cherry	**cerise**		orange	**orange**
grapes	**raisin**		pear	**poire**

Amount **Quantités**

	bouteille		morceau		paquet
	cannette		pot		bouteille
bouteille		paquet		morceau	
cannette		tranche		bouteille	
	tranche		bouteille		morceau
	paquet		tranche		cannette

bottle	**bouteille**		packet	**paquet**
can	**cannette**		piece	**morceau**
jar	**pot**		slice	**tranche**

City **La ville**

visite guidée	métro	taxi	gare		plan
			visite guidée		métro
plan		métro	guide		taxi
taxi		guide	plan		gare
guide		gare			
métro		visite guidée	taxi	gare	guide

station	**gare**	map	**plan**
subway	**métro**	tour guide	**guide**
taxi	**taxi**	tour	**visite guidée**

voyager		passeport	départ		arrivée
					voyager
	voyager	bagages	arrivée		
		billet	passeport	voyager	
billet					
départ		voyager	bagages		billet

to travel	**voyager**		ticket	**billet**
passport	**passeport**		arrival	**arrivée**
luggage	**bagages**		departure	**départ**

The beach **La plage**

bronzer		plonger			
				plonger	
bateau					plonger
		faire du ski nautique	coup de soleil	surfer	
surfer	faire du ski nautique				
coup de soleil		bronzer	surfer		

boat	**bateau**	to surf	**surfer**
to dive	**plonger**	to suntan	**bronzer**
to ski	**faire du ski nautique**	sunburn	**coup de soleil**

The beach La plage

			château de sable	chaud	
soleil	chaud	château de sable		seau	
château de sable		soleil	seau	pelle	
	seau	chaud	soleil		écran solaire
	château de sable		pelle	soleil	seau
	soleil	pelle			

sun	**soleil**	sandcastle	**château de sable**
hot	**chaud**	bucket	**seau**
sunscreen	**écran solaire**	spade	**pelle**

The tour **La visite**

principaux monuments		faire du tourisme			souvenir	
photo		souvenir			appareil photo	
	principaux monuments			souvenir		faire du tourisme
	souvenir			appareil photo		guide
souvenir		principaux monuments			guide	
guide		appareil photo			faire du tourisme	

tour guide	**guide**
photo	**photo**
camera	**appareil photo**

landmark	**principaux monuments**
to go sightseeing	**faire du tourisme**
souvenir	**souvenir**

canard		nourrir	chèvre		poussin
			canard		
chèvre	canard	poussin	nourrir		poule
coq		poule	poussin	chèvre	canard
		coq			
poule		canard	coq		nourrir

duck	**canard**	rooster	**coq**
goat	**chèvre**	chick	**poussin**
hen	**poule**	to feed	**nourrir**

Amusement park Le parc d'attractions

manège	grand huit				grande roue
	faire la queue		grand huit	âge	manège
	âge				
				grande roue	
grand huit	grande roue	ticket		manège	
âge				ticket	grand huit

ticket	**ticket**
age	**âge**
to queue	**faire la queue**

merry-go-round	**manège**
ferris wheel	**grande roue**
roller-coaster	**grand huit**

Camping Le camping

tente			sac à dos	feu de camp	terrain de camping
terrain de camping	sac à dos	feu de camp	tente		
		feu de bois			sac à dos
feu de camp	terrain de camping	sac à dos	feu de bois	tente	sac de couchage
		tente			feu de camp
		terrain de camping			tente

tent	**tente**	sleeping-bag	**sac de couchage**
firewood	**feu de bois**	campsite	**terrain de camping**
backpack	**sac à dos**	campfire	**feu de camp**

At the restaurant Au restaurant

			plat principal		addition			
		plat principal	servir	hors-d'œuvre		menu		additic
table	comman-der	addition				servir		hors-d'œuv
	menu		comman-der					chais
servir			menu	plat principal	dessert			commder
comman-der					table		menu	
addition		servir				chaise	comman-der	table
menu		hors-d'œuvre		comman-der	chaise	addition		
			table		servir			

table	**table**	appetiser	**hors-d'œuvre**	to serve	**servir**
chair	**chaise**	main course	**plat principal**	bill	**addition**
menu	**menu**	dessert	**dessert**	to order	**comman**

				sucré		salé		
salé	sucré	épicé			amer		mou	
	aigre		dur	délicieux		sucré	épicé	amer
aigre	salé		croquant		dur		délicieux	
épicé			amer		aigre		dur	sucré
	amer		sucré	mou	délicieux		salé	épicé
amer	épicé	mou		aigre	croquant		sucré	
	délicieux		salé			mou	amer	croquant
		salé		amer				

salty	**salé**	sour	**aigre**	crunchy	**croquant**
sweet	**sucré**	bitter	**amer**	hard	**dur**
spicy	**épicé**	delicious	**délicieux**	soft	**mou**

Meat and fish Viande et poisson

	porc	poisson					bœuf	
	poulet		porc			calamar	crabe	
saucisse					crevette		porc	poule
porc		bœuf	poulet	crabe		lan-gouste	saucisse	
lan-gouste	crabe	poulet	saucisse		poisson	crevette		bœuf
poisson		saucisse		lan-gouste	bœuf		poulet	crabe
		porc	crabe	saucisse				calamo
	poisson			bœuf	porc			sauciss
crabe	saucisse			crevette				

beef	**bœuf**	sausage	**saucisse**	crab	**crabe**
chicken	**poulet**	fish	**poisson**	lobster	**langouste**
pork	**porc**	shrimp	**crevette**	squid	**calamar**

	riz	soupe				tarte	pizza	
viande rôtie	ragoût			bifteck				pâtes
	produits de la mer			soupe	pizza			
			soupe	pâtes			produits de la mer	
pizza				viande rôtie			ragoût	riz
	viande rôtie	riz					pâtes	tarte
	pizza	bifteck		tarte		ragoût	riz	
produits de la mer	tarte						viande rôtie	pizza
	soupe	viande rôtie		pizza	bifteck	produits de la mer	pâtes	

soup	**soupe**	pasta	**pâtes**	pie	**tarte**
roast meat	**viande rôtie**	steak	**bifteck**	stew	**ragoût**
rice	**riz**	pizza	**pizza**	seafood	**produits de la mer**

Fruit Les fruits

noix de coco	melon			banane		cerise	pample-mousse	
	pample-mousse			pêche			noix de coco	kiwi
raisin						abricot	melon	
banane		cerise	melon		pêche			raisin
	pêche	pample-mousse				banane	apricot	
kiwi			banane		noix de coco	melon		
	kiwi	abricot						pample-mousse
pample-mousse	raisin			cerise			banane	
	banane	melon		noix de coco			raisin	abricot

apricot	**abricot**	grapefruit	**pample-mousse**	cherry	**cerise**
banana	**banane**			grapes	**raisin**
peach	**pêche**	melon	**melon**	kiwi	**kiwi**
		coconut	**noix de coco**		

Vegetables **Les légumes**

					betterave	maïs	poireau	
	céleri		poireau			betterave	poivron	
poireau	poivron		maïs		haricots		asperge	céleri
	maïs	poivron		haricots		épinard	betterave	asperge
asperge								maïs
épinard	betterave			maïs		poireau	concombre	
betterave	asperge		épinard		poivron		maïs	poireau
	poireau	concombre			asperge			
	haricots	épinard	betterave					

celery	**céleri**	corn	**maïs**	cucumber	**concombre**
leek	**poireau**	spinach	**épinard**	beetroot	**betterave**
pepper	**poivron**	asparagus	**asperge**	beans	**haricots**

Cooking **Cuisiner**

huile		beurre		sucre	cuisiner	piment	sel	farine
	cuisiner			huile				sucre
sel					lait	beurre	cuisiner	huile
		lait		cuisiner	sucre	sel	beurre	piment
	piment	cuisiner				farine		
sucre	farine	sel	beurre	lait		huile		
lait	beurre	huile	cuisiner					sel
cuisiner				beurre			huile	
farine	sucre	vinaigre	lait	sel		cuisiner		beurre

to cook	**cuisiner**	butter	**beurre**	oil	**huile**
salt	**sel**	milk	**lait**	vinegar	**vinaigre**
sugar	**sucre**	flour	**farine**	chilli	**piment**

ocolats	cacahuètes		pop-corn	chips	sucette		biscuit	guimauve
chips			chocolats			pop-corn	sucreries	
	pop-corn		sucreries	biscuit				
ucette	guimauve	chips		cacahuètes		biscuit		
iscuit	chocolats						cacahuètes	gâteau
	gâteau	cacahuètes		pop-corn		guimauve	chocolats	sucette
				sucreries	guimauve		sucette	
	sucette	chocolats			chips			biscuit
imauve	sucreries		sucette	chocolats	pop-corn		gâteau	chips

ocolates **chocolats**   peanuts **cacahuètes**   marshmallow **guimauve**

pcorn **pop-corn**   lollipop **sucette**   cake **gâteau**

tato crisps **chips**   sweets **sucreries**   biscuit **biscuit**

Level 3: Vacations

The beach La plage

palmier				île		palmes		coquilla
	surveillant de baignade	tuba				étoile de mer	île	
	méduse	coquillage	palmier	étoile de mer			tuba	
surveillant de baignade	île	palmes	étoile de mer			tuba		
jetée		palmier	méduse	surveillant de baignade		île	coquillage	
					jetée	surveillant de baignade	palmier	étoile de mer
	tuba		jetée				palmes	
coquillage	palmes		surveillant de baignade	méduse		palmier		
					coquillage			jetée

flippers **palmes** starfish **étoile de mer** palm tree **palmie**
snorkel **tuba** lifeguard **surveillant de baignade** pier **jetée**
seashell **coquillage** jellyfish **méduse** island **île**

	neige		bonhomme de neige	écharpe	gants			ski
			patin à glace			glace		
ski	gants	écharpe				bonhomme de neige		patin à glace
charpe		gants	bottes		ski			
glace	bottes			neige	bonhomme de neige			
						patin à glace	boule de neige	
gants	ski		boule de neige	glace		bottes		bonhomme de neige
							glace	neige
nhomme de neige		patin à glace				écharpe	gants	boule de neige

snow	**neige**	skiing	**ski**	scarf	**écharpe**
ice	**glace**	boots	**bottes**	snowball	**boule de neige**
ice-skating	**patin à glace**	gloves	**gants**	snowman	**bonhomme de neige**

47

In the mountains À la montagne

montagne			falaise	vallée		cascade	colline	
		colline	rivière	lac			montagne	
			colline	montagne	source chaude	vallée	lac	randonée
	falaise	vallée			montagne			collin
source chaude		rivière				falaise		montag
randonnée			source chaude			rivière	cascade	
lac	cascade	falaise	montagne	randonnée	rivière			
	montagne			falaise	vallée	randonnée		
	vallée	randonnée		source chaude	colline			lac

mountain	**montagne**	valley	**vallée**	hot spring	**source chaude**
hill	**colline**	lake	**lac**	waterfall	**cascade**
cliff	**falaise**	river	**rivière**	hike	**randonn**

rrivée	billet	quai	train	immigration	annulé			douanes
	train			quai	départ			
	départ	immigration		douanes	retardé			arrivée
train			quai	départ		billet	retardé	
			annulé	arrivée			train	
quai			retardé	train	douanes	départ	arrivée	immigration
	quai	départ			train			retardé
uanes		annulé				quai		train
migration			douanes	retardé		annulé	billet	

ival	**arrivée**	immigration	**immigration**	cancelled	**annulé**
parture	**départ**	ticket	**billet**	train	**train**
stoms	**douanes**	delayed	**retardé**	platform	**quai**

City La ville

pont					fontaine	cinéma	horloge	squar
square	fontaine		horloge				parc	
horloge	tour	parc	square				fontaine	musé
tour		pont		cinéma	horloge		square	fontair
théâtre		fontaine	musée	parc		pont		
musée	cinéma		pont		tour	parc		
cinéma	square			musée				
	théâtre	musée			pont	square	tour	
parc		horloge			théâtre	fontaine	musée	ciném

bridge	**pont**	tower	**tour**	cinema	**cinéma**
square	**square**	theatre	**théâtre**	fountain	**fontaine**
clock	**horloge**	museum	**musée**	park	**parc**

50

nvelo-ppe	envoyer	carte postale	lettre					recevoir
	adresse		carte postale	recevoir		envoyer		
	recevoir	lire	envoyer	écrire	adresse	carte postale		
	carte postale	recevoir	écrire		lettre		enveloppe	envoyer
ettre			timbre		recevoir	lire	adresse	
resse			lire	enveloppe		lettre		écrire
			enveloppe	carte postale			lire	
carte ostale	écrire			timbre	lire			lettre
cevoir	lire	enveloppe	adresse		envoyer			timbre

nvelope	**enveloppe**	postcard	**carte postale**	to receive	**recevoir**
ddress	**adresse**			to send	**envoyer**
tter	**lettre**	stamp	**timbre**	to write	**écrire**
		to read	**lire**		

Summer L'été

	glace	ballon	bronzer	faire du vélo		transpirer	piscine	lunette de sole(il)
piscine		transpirer			nager		faire du vélo	
faire du vélo			lunettes de soleil					nage(r)
plage		piscine		bronzer			nager	
bronzer	faire du vélo			ballon	glace	piscine	lunettes de soleil	transpi(rer)
					transpirer	faire du vélo		bronz(er)
lunettes de soleil	piscine			plage			ballon	
					ballon		bronzer	
ballon	plage	bronzer	nager	piscine			transpirer	glace

beach	**plage**	ball	**ballon**
pool	**piscine**	ice cream	**glace**
sunglasses	**lunettes de soleil**	to cycle	**faire du vélo**

to sweat	**transpir(er)**
to suntan	**bronzer**
to swim	**nager**

				écharpe	tongs		sandales	bottes
bikini	cas-quette	bottes						
				bottes			maillot de bain	cas-quette
maillot de bain	slip de bain	écharpe		bikini	sandales	cas-quette		
						tongs		maillot de bain
tongs		cas-quette	slip de bain		maillot de bain			
sandales					cas-quette		tongs	bikini
bottes	gants				écharpe			
		slip de bain	bottes	maillot de bain	bikini	gants		sandales

kini	**bikini**	flip-flops	**tongs**	gloves	**gants**
vimsuit	**maillot de bain**	sandals	**sandales**	scarf	**écharpe**
nks	**slip de bain**	boots	**bottes**	cap	**casquette**

Meals

...er	déjeuner	casse-croûte	petit déjeuner
...se-ûte	petit déjeuner	dîner	déjeuner
...tit ...uner	casse-croûte	déjeuner	dîner
...uner	dîner	petit déjeuner	casse-croûte

p. 6 To eat and drink

boisson	aliments	boire	manger
manger	boire	boisson	aliments
boire	manger	aliments	boisson
aliments	boisson	manger	boire

p. 7 On the table

fourchette	couteau	serviette	cuiller
cuiller	serviette	couteau	fourchette
couteau	cuiller	fourchette	serviette
serviette	fourchette	cuiller	couteau

Condiments

...vre	sel	huile d'olive	vinaigre
...le ...ve	vinaigre	poivre	sel
...l	poivre	vinaigre	huile d'olive
...igre	huile d'olive	sel	poivre

p. 8 Where to buy things

supérette	drugstore	super-marché	centre commercial
centre commercial	super-marché	drugstore	supérette
super-marché	centre commercial	supérette	drugstore
drugstore	supérette	centre commercial	super-marché

p. 8 Where to eat

pub	snack-bar	restaurant	café
restaurant	café	pub	snack-bar
snack-bar	pub	café	restaurant
café	restaurant	snack-bar	pub

Breakfast

...in	céréales	yaourt	muffin
...urt	muffin	pain	céréales
...ffin	yaourt	céréales	pain
...ales	pain	muffin	yaourt

p. 9 Breakfast

fromage	confiture	miel	beurre
miel	beurre	fromage	confiture
beurre	miel	confiture	fromage
confiture	fromage	beurre	miel

p. 10 Nuts

cacahuète	noix de cajou	noix	amande
noix	amande	noix de cajou	cacahuète
noix de cajou	cacahuète	amande	noix
amande	noix	cacahuète	noix de cajou

p. 10 Vegetables

ail	oignon	carotte	tomate
tomate	carotte	oignon	ail
carotte	tomate	ail	oignon
oignon	ail	tomate	carotte

p. 11 Meat

viande	poulet	bœuf	porc
bœuf	porc	poulet	viande
poulet	viande	porc	bœuf
porc	bœuf	viande	poulet

p. 11 Seafood

calamar	crustacés	crevette	pois
poisson	crevette	crustacés	cal
crustacés	calamar	poisson	crev
crevette	poisson	calamar	crus

p. 12 Food

hors-d'œuvre	plat principal	soupe	salade
salade	soupe	plat principal	hors-d'œuvre
plat principal	salade	hors-d'œuvre	soupe
soupe	hors-d'œuvre	salade	plat principal

p. 12 Dessert

gâteau	fruit	gelée	glace
gelée	glace	gâteau	fruit
glace	gelée	fruit	gâteau
fruit	gâteau	glace	gelée

p. 13 Drinks

jus de fruit	thé	lait	c
café	lait	thé	jus d
thé	jus de fruit	café	l
lait	café	jus de fruit	t

p. 13 Drinks

bière	eau	vin	boisson sans alcool
vin	boisson sans alcool	bière	eau
boisson sans alcool	bière	eau	vin
eau	vin	boisson sans alcool	bière

NOTES:

Solutions - Level 1

4 Trips

voyager	passeport	vacances	
passeport	hôtel	voyager	
vacances	voyager	hôtel	
hôtel	vacances	passeport	

p. 14 Destinations

plage	montagne	ville	lac
ville	lac	plage	montagne
montagne	ville	lac	plage
lac	plage	montagne	ville

p. 15 The hotel

chambre	réception	douche	toilettes
douche	toilettes	chambre	réception
réception	chambre	toilettes	douche
toilettes	douche	réception	chambre

5 Luggage

bagages	sac à dos	bagage à main	
sac à dos	bagages	valise	
valise	bagage à main	sac à dos	
bagage à main	valise	bagages	

p. 16 Car

conduire	embouteillage	ceinture de sécurité	conducteur
ceinture de sécurité	conducteur	conduire	embouteillage
conducteur	conduire	embouteillage	ceinture de sécurité
embouteillage	ceinture de sécurité	conducteur	conduire

p. 16 Plane

décoller	atterrir	embarquement	siège
embarquement	siège	décoller	atterrir
atterrir	embarquement	siège	décoller
siège	décoller	atterrir	embarquement

7 The farm

vache	lapin	mouton	
mouton	cheval	vache	
lapin	mouton	cheval	
cheval	vache	lapin	

p. 17 Rain

pluie	imperméable	parapluie	blouson
parapluie	blouson	pluie	imperméable
blouson	pluie	imperméable	parapluie
imperméable	parapluie	blouson	pluie

p. 18 Family

père	mère	fils	fille
fils	fille	mère	père
fille	fils	père	mère
mère	père	fille	fils

p. 18 The playground

balançoire	bascule	toboggan	échelle
échelle	toboggan	bascule	balançoire
bascule	balançoire	échelle	toboggan
toboggan	échelle	balançoire	bascule

p. 19 Playing

sauter	rire	courir	jouer
jouer	courir	rire	sauter
courir	jouer	sauter	rire
rire	sauter	jouer	courir

p. 19 Swimming

tongs	maillot de bain	bikini	slip b...
slip de bain	bikini	tongs	mail b...
bikini	slip de bain	maillot de bain	to...
maillot de bain	tongs	slip de bain	bi...

p. 20 Travel

autobus	voiture	avion	bateau
bateau	avion	autobus	voiture
voiture	autobus	bateau	avion
avion	bateau	voiture	autobus

p. 20 The beach

sable	vague	soleil	mer
soleil	mer	sable	vague
mer	soleil	vague	sable
vague	sable	mer	soleil

p. 21 Family and frie...

coloca-taire	copain	famille	c...
ami	famille	coloca-taire	co...
copain	coloca-taire	ami	fa...
famille	ami	copain	co... t...

p. 21 The farm

poney	ferme	tracteur	champ
champ	tracteur	ferme	poney
ferme	champ	poney	tracteur
tracteur	poney	champ	ferme

NOTES:

Solutions - Level 2

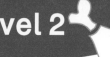

22 On the table

rre	couteau	fourchette	cuiller	table	assiette
ble	cuiller	assiette	fourchette	verre	couteau
ller	assiette	couteau	table	fourchette	verre
chette	verre	table	assiette	couteau	cuiller
teau	fourchette	cuiller	verre	assiette	table
iette	table	verre	couteau	cuiller	fourchette

p. 23 At the restaurant

serveur	comman-der	servir	menu	addition	serveuse
addition	serveuse	menu	comman-der	servir	serveur
servir	addition	serveuse	serveur	comman-der	menu
comman-der	menu	serveur	addition	serveuse	servir
serveuse	serveur	addition	servir	menu	comman-der
menu	servir	comman-der	serveuse	serveur	addition

24 Vegetables

colis	navet	chou-fleur	aubergine	potiron	chou
rgine	potiron	chou	broccolis	navet	chou-fleur
vet	chou-fleur	broccolis	potiron	chou	aubergine
ron	chou	aubergine	navet	chou-fleur	broccolis
-fleur	broccolis	navet	chou	aubergine	potiron
ou	aubergine	potiron	chou-fleur	broccolis	navet

p. 25 Meat

agneau	bifteck	bacon	dinde	saucisse	hambur-ger
saucisse	hambur-ger	dinde	bifteck	agneau	bacon
dinde	saucisse	hambur-ger	bacon	bifteck	agneau
bacon	agneau	bifteck	saucisse	hambur-ger	dinde
bifteck	bacon	agneau	hambur-ger	dinde	saucisse
hambur-ger	dinde	saucisse	agneau	bacon	bifteck

NOTES:

p. 26 Dishes

hot-dog	hamburger	spaghetti	omelette	tarte	soupe
tarte	omelette	soupe	hamburger	spaghetti	hot-dog
spaghetti	soupe	hot-dog	tarte	hamburger	omelette
hamburger	tarte	omelette	soupe	hot-dog	spaghetti
omelette	spaghetti	hamburger	hot-dog	soupe	tarte
soupe	hot-dog	tarte	spaghetti	omelette	hamburger

p. 27 Sandwich

ketchup	laitue	œuf	tomate	jambon	frome
fromage	jambon	tomate	laitue	ketchup	œu
tomate	œuf	laitue	jambon	fromage	ketc
jambon	fromage	ketchup	œuf	laitue	tom
laitue	tomate	fromage	ketchup	œuf	jamb
œuf	ketchup	jambon	fromage	tomate	lait

p. 28 Fruit

orange	poire	citron	raisin	cerise	pomme
pomme	cerise	raisin	poire	orange	citron
cerise	raisin	pomme	orange	citron	poire
citron	orange	poire	cerise	pomme	raisin
poire	citron	cerise	pomme	raisin	orange
raisin	pomme	orange	citron	poire	cerise

p. 29 Amount

tranche	bouteille	pot	morceau	cannette	paq
paquet	cannette	morceau	pot	tranche	boute
bouteille	pot	paquet	cannette	morceau	tran
cannette	morceau	tranche	paquet	bouteille	po
pot	tranche	cannette	bouteille	paquet	mor
morceau	paquet	bouteille	tranche	pot	cann

NOTES:

Solutions - Level 2

30 City

visite guidée	métro	taxi	gare	guide	plan
gare	guide	plan	visite guidée	taxi	métro
plan	gare	métro	guide	visite guidée	taxi
taxi	visite guidée	guide	plan	métro	gare
guide	taxi	gare	métro	plan	visite guidée
métro	plan	visite guidée	taxi	gare	guide

p. 31 Travel

voyager	billet	passeport	départ	bagages	arrivée
bagages	arrivée	départ	billet	passeport	voyager
passeport	voyager	bagages	arrivée	billet	départ
arrivée	départ	billet	passeport	voyager	bagages
billet	bagages	arrivée	voyager	départ	passeport
départ	passeport	voyager	bagages	arrivée	billet

32 The beach

bronzer	coup de soleil	plonger	bateau	faire du ski nautique	surfer
faire du ski nautique	bateau	surfer	plonger	coup de soleil	bronzer
bateau	surfer	coup de soleil	faire du ski nautique	bronzer	plonger
plonger	bronzer	faire du ski nautique	coup de soleil	surfer	bateau
surfer	faire du ski nautique	bateau	bronzer	plonger	coup de soleil
coup de soleil	plonger	bronzer	surfer	bateau	faire du ski nautique

p. 33 The beach

écran solaire	pelle	seau	château de sable	chaud	soleil
soleil	chaud	château de sable	écran solaire	seau	pelle
château de sable	écran solaire	soleil	seau	pelle	chaud
pelle	seau	chaud	soleil	château de sable	écran solaire
chaud	château de sable	écran solaire	pelle	soleil	seau
seau	soleil	pelle	chaud	écran solaire	château de sable

NOTES:

p. 34 The tour

principaux monuments	appareil photo	faire du tourisme	guide	souvenir	photo
photo	guide	souvenir	faire du tourisme	appareil photo	principaux monuments
appareil photo	principaux monuments	guide	souvenir	photo	faire du tourisme
faire du tourisme	souvenir	photo	appareil photo	principaux monuments	guide
souvenir	faire du tourisme	principaux monuments	photo	guide	appareil photo
guide	photo	appareil photo	principaux monuments	faire du tourisme	souvenir

p. 35 The farm

canard	coq	nourrir	chèvre	poule	pous
poussin	poule	chèvre	canard	nourrir	co
chèvre	canard	poussin	nourrir	coq	pou
coq	nourrir	poule	poussin	chèvre	can
nourrir	poussin	coq	poule	canard	chè
poule	chèvre	canard	coq	poussin	nou

p. 36 Amusement park

manège	grand huit	âge	ticket	faire la queue	grande roue
ticket	faire la queue	grande roue	grand huit	âge	manège
grande roue	âge	manège	faire la queue	grand huit	ticket
faire la queue	ticket	grand huit	manège	grande roue	âge
grand huit	grande roue	ticket	âge	manège	faire la queue
âge	manège	faire la queue	grande roue	ticket	grand huit

p. 37 Camping

tente	feu de bois	sac de couchage	sac à dos	feu de camp	terra cam
terrain de camping	sac à dos	feu de camp	tente	sac de couchage	feu bo
sac de couchage	tente	feu de bois	feu de camp	terrain de camping	sac à
feu de camp	terrain de camping	sac à dos	feu de bois	tente	sac couc
sac à dos	sac de couchage	tente	terrain de camping	feu de bois	feu ca
feu de bois	feu de camp	terrain de camping	sac de couchage	sac à dos	ter

NOTES:

Solutions - Level 3

p. 38 At the restaurant

hors-d'œuvre	servir	menu	plat principal	table	addition	commander	chaise	dessert
dessert	chaise	plat principal	servir	hors-d'œuvre	commander	menu	table	addition
table	commander	addition	chaise	dessert	menu	servir	plat principal	hors-d'œuvre
plat principal	menu	table	commander	servir	hors-d'œuvre	dessert	addition	chaise
servir	addition	chaise	menu	plat principal	dessert	table	hors-d'œuvre	commander
commander	hors-d'œuvre	dessert	addition	chaise	table	plat principal	menu	servir
addition	dessert	servir	hors-d'œuvre	menu	plat principal	chaise	commander	table
menu	table	hors-d'œuvre	dessert	commander	chaise	addition	servir	plat principal
chaise	plat principal	commander	table	addition	servir	hors-d'œuvre	dessert	menu

p. 39 Taste

délicieux	dur	amer	épicé	sucré	mou	salé	croquant	aigre
salé	sucré	épicé	aigre	croquant	amer	délicieux	mou	dur
mou	aigre	croquant	dur	délicieux	salé	sucré	épicé	amer
aigre	salé	sucré	croquant	épicé	dur	amer	délicieux	mou
épicé	mou	délicieux	amer	salé	aigre	croquant	dur	sucré
croquant	amer	dur	sucré	mou	délicieux	aigre	salé	épicé
amer	épicé	mou	délicieux	aigre	croquant	dur	sucré	salé
sucré	délicieux	aigre	salé	dur	épicé	mou	amer	croquant
dur	croquant	salé	mou	amer	sucré	épicé	aigre	délicieux

p. 40 Meat and fish

calamar	porc	poisson	langouste	poulet	crabe	saucisse	bœuf	crevette
bœuf	poulet	crevette	porc	poisson	saucisse	calamar	crabe	langouste
saucisse	langouste	crabe	bœuf	calamar	crevette	poisson	porc	poulet
porc	crevette	bœuf	poulet	crabe	calamar	langouste	saucisse	poisson
langouste	crabe	poulet	saucisse	porc	poisson	crevette	calamar	bœuf
poisson	calamar	saucisse	crevette	langouste	bœuf	porc	poulet	crabe
crevette	bœuf	porc	crabe	saucisse	langouste	poulet	poisson	calamar
poulet	poisson	langouste	calamar	bœuf	porc	crabe	crevette	saucisse
crabe	saucisse	calamar	poisson	crevette	poulet	bœuf	langouste	porc

p. 41 Dishes

bifteck	riz	soupe	viande rôtie	ragoût	pâtes	tarte	pizza	produits de la mer
viande rôtie	ragoût	pizza	tarte	bifteck	produits de la mer	riz	soupe	pâtes
tarte	produits de la mer	pâtes	riz	soupe	pizza	viande rôtie	bifteck	ragoût
ragoût	bifteck	tarte	soupe	pâtes	riz	pizza	produits de la mer	viande rôtie
pizza	pâtes	produits de la mer	bifteck	viande rôtie	tarte	soupe	ragoût	riz
soupe	viande rôtie	riz	pizza	produits de la mer	ragoût	pâtes	tarte	bifteck
pâtes	pizza	bifteck	produits de la mer	tarte	viande rôtie	ragoût	riz	soupe
produits de la mer	tarte	ragoût	pâtes	riz	soupe	bifteck	viande rôtie	pizza
riz	soupe	viande rôtie	ragoût	pizza	bifteck	produits de la mer	pâtes	tarte

p. 42 Fruit

noix de coco	melon	kiwi	abricot	banane	raisin	cerise	pample-mousse	pêche
abricot	pample-mousse	banane	cerise	pêche	melon	raisin	noix de coco	kiwi
raisin	cerise	pêche	noix de coco	kiwi	pample-mousse	abricot	melon	banane
banane	noix de coco	cerise	melon	abricot	pêche	pample-mousse	kiwi	raisin
melon	pêche	pample-mousse	kiwi	raisin	cerise	banane	abricot	noix de coco
kiwi	abricot	raisin	banane	pample-mousse	noix de coco	melon	pêche	cerise
pêche	kiwi	abricot	raisin	melon	banane	noix de coco	cerise	pample-mousse
pample-mousse	raisin	noix de coco	pêche	cerise	abricot	kiwi	banane	melon
cerise	banane	melon	pample-mousse	noix de coco	kiwi	pêche	raisin	abricot

p. 43 Vegetables

concom-bre	épinard	asperge	céleri	poivron	bette-rave	maïs	poireau	haricots
haricots	céleri	maïs	poireau	asperge	concom-bre	bette-rave	poivron	épinard
poireau	poivron	bette-rave	maïs	épinard	haricots	concom-bre	asperge	céleri
céleri	maïs	poivron	concom-bre	haricots	poireau	épinard	bette-rave	asperge
asperge	concom-bre	poireau	poivron	bette-rave	épinard	céleri	haricots	maïs
épinard	bette-rave	haricots	asperge	maïs	céleri	poireau	concom-bre	poivron
bette-rave	asperge	céleri	épinard	concom-bre	poivron	haricots	maïs	poireau
maïs	poireau	concom-bre	haricots	céleri	asperge	poivron	épinard	bette-rave
poivron	haricots	épinard	bette-rave	poireau	maïs	asperge	céleri	concom-bre

p. 44 Cooking

huile	lait	beurre	vinaigre	sucre	cuisiner	piment	sel	farine
piment	cuisiner	farine	sel	huile	beurre	vinaigre	lait	sucre
sel	vinaigre	sucre	piment	farine	lait	beurre	cuisiner	huile
vinaigre	huile	lait	farine	cuisiner	sucre	sel	beurre	piment
beurre	piment	cuisiner	huile	vinaigre	sel	farine	sucre	lait
sucre	farine	sel	beurre	lait	piment	huile	vinaigre	cuisiner
lait	beurre	huile	cuisiner	piment	vinaigre	sucre	farine	sel
cuisiner	sel	piment	sucre	beurre	farine	lait	huile	vinaigre
farine	sucre	vinaigre	lait	sel	huile	cuisiner	piment	beurre

p. 45 Party food

chocolats	cacahuètes	sucreries	pop-corn	chips	sucette	gâteau	biscuit	guimauve
chips	biscuit	sucette	chocolats	guimauve	gâteau	pop-corn	sucreries	cacahuètes
gâteau	pop-corn	guimauve	sucreries	biscuit	cacahuètes	sucette	chips	chocolats
sucette	guimauve	chips	gâteau	cacahuètes	chocolats	biscuit	pop-corn	sucreries
biscuit	chocolats	pop-corn	guimauve	sucette	sucreries	chips	cacahuètes	gâteau
sucreries	gâteau	cacahuètes	chips	pop-corn	biscuit	guimauve	chocolats	sucette
cacahuètes	chips	gâteau	biscuit	sucreries	guimauve	chocolats	sucette	pop-corn
pop-corn	sucette	chocolats	cacahuètes	gâteau	chips	sucreries	guimauve	biscuit
guimauve	sucreries	biscuit	sucette	chocolats	pop-corn	cacahuètes	gâteau	chips

p. 46 The beach

palmier	jetée	étoile de mer	tuba	île	surveillant de baignade	palmes	méduse	coquillage
palmes	surveillant de baignade	tuba	coquillage	jetée	méduse	étoile de mer	île	palmier
île	méduse	coquillage	palmier	étoile de mer	palmes	jetée	tuba	surveillant de baignade
surveillant de baignade	île	palmes	étoile de mer	coquillage	palmier	tuba	jetée	méduse
jetée	étoile de mer	palmier	méduse	surveillant de baignade	tuba	île	coquillage	palmes
tuba	coquillage	méduse	île	palmes	jetée	surveillant de baignade	palmier	étoile de mer
méduse	tuba	surveillant de baignade	jetée	palmier	étoile de mer	coquillage	palmes	île
coquillage	palmes	jetée	surveillant de baignade	méduse	île	palmier	étoile de mer	tuba
étoile de mer	palmier	île	palmes	tuba	coquillage	méduse	surveillant de baignade	jetée

p. 47 Winter

patin à glace	neige	glace	bonhomme de neige	écharpe	gants	boule de neige	bottes	ski
bottes	boule de neige	bonhomme de neige	ski	patin à glace	neige	glace	écharpe	gants
ski	gants	écharpe	glace	bottes	boule de neige	bonhomme de neige	neige	patin à glace
écharpe	patin à glace	gants	bottes	boule de neige	ski	neige	bonhomme de neige	glace
glace	bottes	boule de neige	patin à glace	neige	bonhomme de neige	gants	ski	écharpe
neige	bonhomme de neige	ski	écharpe	gants	glace	patin à glace	boule de neige	bottes
gants	ski	neige	boule de neige	glace	écharpe	bottes	patin à glace	bonhomme de neige
boule de neige	écharpe	bottes	gants	bonhomme de neige	patin à glace	ski	glace	neige
bonhomme de neige	glace	patin à glace	neige	ski	bottes	écharpe	gants	boule de neige

p. 48 In the mountains

monta-gne	source chaude	lac	falaise	vallée	randon-née	cascade	colline	rivière
vallée	randon-née	colline	rivière	lac	cascade	source chaude	monta-gne	falaise
falaise	rivière	cascade	colline	monta-gne	source chaude	vallée	lac	randon-née
cascade	falaise	vallée	randon-née	rivière	monta-gne	lac	source chaude	colline
source chaude	colline	rivière	vallée	cascade	lac	falaise	randon-née	monta-gne
randon-née	lac	monta-gne	source chaude	colline	falaise	rivière	cascade	vallée
lac	cascade	falaise	monta-gne	randon-née	rivière	colline	vallée	source chaude
colline	monta-gne	source chaude	lac	falaise	vallée	randon-née	rivière	cascade
rivière	vallée	randon-née	cascade	source chaude	colline	monta-gne	falaise	lac

p. 49 Travel

arrivée	billet	quai	train	immi-gration	annulé	retardé	départ	douanes
retardé	train	douanes	arrivée	quai	départ	immi-gration	annulé	billet
annulé	départ	immi-gration	billet	douanes	retardé	train	quai	arrivée
train	douanes	arrivée	quai	départ	immi-gration	billet	retardé	annulé
départ	immi-gration	retardé	annulé	arrivée	billet	douanes	train	quai
quai	annulé	billet	retardé	train	douanes	départ	arrivée	immi-gration
billet	quai	départ	immi-gration	annulé	train	arrivée	douanes	retardé
douanes	retardé	annulé	départ	billet	arrivée	quai	immi-gration	train
immi-gration	arrivée	train	douanes	retardé	quai	annulé	billet	départ

p. 50 City

pont	musée	théâtre	parc	tour	fontaine	cinéma	horloge	square
square	fontaine	cinéma	horloge	théâtre	musée	tour	parc	pont
horloge	tour	parc	square	pont	cinéma	théâtre	fontaine	musée
tour	parc	pont	théâtre	cinéma	horloge	musée	square	fontaine
théâtre	horloge	fontaine	musée	parc	square	pont	cinéma	tour
musée	cinéma	square	pont	fontaine	tour	parc	théâtre	horloge
cinéma	square	tour	fontaine	musée	parc	horloge	pont	théâtre
fontaine	théâtre	musée	cinéma	horloge	pont	square	tour	parc
parc	pont	horloge	tour	square	théâtre	fontaine	musée	cinéma

p. 51 Postcards

enveloppe	envoyer	carte postale	lettre	lire	timbre	adresse	écrire	recevoir
écrire	adresse	lettre	carte postale	recevoir	enveloppe	envoyer	timbre	lire
timbre	recevoir	lire	envoyer	écrire	adresse	carte postale	lettre	enveloppe
lire	carte postale	recevoir	écrire	adresse	lettre	timbre	enveloppe	envoyer
lettre	enveloppe	écrire	timbre	envoyer	recevoir	lire	adresse	carte postale
adresse	timbre	envoyer	lire	enveloppe	carte postale	lettre	recevoir	écrire
envoyer	lettre	timbre	enveloppe	carte postale	écrire	recevoir	lire	adresse
carte postale	écrire	adresse	recevoir	timbre	lire	enveloppe	envoyer	lettre
recevoir	lire	enveloppe	adresse	lettre	envoyer	écrire	carte postale	timbre

p. 52 Summer

nager	glace	ballon	bronzer	faire du vélo	plage	transpi-rer	piscine	lunettes de soleil
piscine	lunettes de soleil	transpi-rer	ballon	glace	nager	bronzer	faire du vélo	plage
faire du vélo	bronzer	plage	lunettes de soleil	transpi-rer	piscine	ballon	glace	nager
plage	transpi-rer	piscine	faire du vélo	bronzer	lunettes de soleil	glace	nager	ballon
bronzer	faire du vélo	nager	plage	ballon	glace	piscine	lunettes de soleil	transpi-rer
glace	ballon	lunettes de soleil	piscine	nager	transpi-rer	faire du vélo	plage	bronzer
lunettes de soleil	piscine	glace	transpi-rer	plage	bronzer	nager	ballon	faire du vélo
transpi-rer	nager	faire du vélo	glace	lunettes de soleil	ballon	plage	bronzer	piscine
ballon	plage	bronzer	nager	piscine	faire du vélo	lunettes de soleil	transpi-rer	glace

p. 53 Clothing

slip de bain	maillot de bain	gants	cas-quette	écharpe	tongs	bikini	sanda-les	bottes
bikini	cas-quette	bottes	maillot de bain	sanda-les	slip de bain	écharpe	gants	tongs
écharpe	sanda-les	tongs	bikini	bottes	gants	slip de bain	maillot de bain	cas-quette
maillot de bain	slip de bain	écharpe	tongs	bikini	sanda-les	cas-quette	bottes	gants
gants	bikini	sanda-les	écharpe	cas-quette	bottes	tongs	slip de bain	maillot de bain
tongs	bottes	cas-quette	slip de bain	gants	maillot de bain	sanda-les	bikini	écharpe
sanda-les	écharpe	maillot de bain	gants	slip de bain	cas-quette	bottes	tongs	bikini
bottes	gants	bikini	sanda-les	tongs	écharpe	maillot de bain	cas-quette	slip de bain
cas-quette	tongs	slip de bain	bottes	maillot de bain	bikini	gants	écharpe	sanda-les

INDEX

address; p.51
age; p.36
almond; p.10
appetiser; p.12, 38
apple; p.28
apricot; p.42
arrival; p.31, 49
asparagus; p.43
backpack; p.15, 37
bacon; p.25
bag; p.15
ball; p.52
banana; p.42
beach; p.14, 52
beans; p.43
beef; p.11, 40
beer; p.13
beetroot; p.43
beverage; p.6
bikini; p.19, 53
bill; p.23, 38
biscuit; p.45
bitter; p.39
boarding; p.16
boat; p.20, 32
boots; p.47, 53
bottle; p.29
bread; p.9
breakfast; p.6
bridge; p.50
broccoli; p.24
bucket; p.33
buddy; p.21
bus; p.20
butter; p.9, 44
cabbage; p.24
café; p.8
cake; p.12, 45
camera; p.34
campfire; p.37
campsite; p.37
can; p.29
cancelled; p.49
cap; p.53
car; p.20
carrot; p.10
cashew nut; p.10
cauliflower; p.24
celery; p.43
cereal; p.9
chair; p.38
cheese; p.9, 27

cherry; p.28, 42
chick; p.35
chicken; p.11, 40
chilli; p.44
chocolates; p.45
cinema; p.50
city; p.14
cliff; p.48
clock; p.50
coconut; p.42
coffee; p.13
convenience store; p.8
corn; p.43
cow; p.17
crab; p.40
crunchy; p.39
cucumber; p.43
customs; p.49
daughter; p.18
delayed; p.49
delicious; p.39
departure; p.31, 49
dessert; p.38
dinner; p.6
driver; p.16
drugstore; p.8
duck; p.35
egg; p.27
eggplant; p.24
envelope; p.51
family; p.21
farm; p.21
father; p.18
ferris wheel; p.36
field; p.21
firewood; p.37
fish; p.11, 40
flatmate; p.21
flip-flops; p.19, 53
flippers; p.46
flour; p.44
food; p.6
fork; p.7, 22
fountain; p.50
friend; p.21
fruit; p.12
garlic; p.10
glass; p.22
gloves; p.47, 53
goat; p.35
grapefruit; p.42
grapes; p.28, 42

ham; p.27
hamburger; p.25, 26
hand luggage; p.15
hard; p.39
hen; p.35
hike; p.48
hill; p.48
honey; p.9
horse; p.17
hot; p.33
hot dog; p.26
hot spring; p.48
hotel; p.14
ice; p.47
ice cream; p.12, 52
ice-skating; p.47
immigration; p.49
island; p.46
jacket; p.17
jam; p.9
jar; p.29
jelly; p.12
jellyfish; p.46
juice; p.13
ketchup; p.27
kiwi; p.42
knife; p.7, 22
ladder; p.18
lake; p.14, 48
lamb; p.25
landmark; p.34
leek; p.43
lemon; p.28
letter; p.51
lettuce; p.27
lifeguard; p.46
lobby; p.15
lobster; p.40
lollipop; p.45
luggage; p.15, 31
lunch; p.6
main course; p.12, 38
mall; p.8
map; p.30
marshmallow; p.45
meat; p.11
melon; p.42
menu; p.23, 38
merry-go-round; p.36
milk; p.13, 44
mother; p.18
mountain; p.14, 48

INDEX

muffin; p.9
museum; p.50
napkin; p.7
oil; p.44
olive oil; p.7
omelette; p.26
onion; p.10
orange; p.28
packet; p.29
palm tree; p.46
park; p.50
passport; p.14, 31
pasta; p.41
peach; p.42
peanut; p.10
peanuts; p.45
pear; p.28
pepper; p.7, 43
photo; p.34
pie; p.26, 41
piece; p.29
pier; p.46
pizza; p.41
plane; p.20
plate; p.22
platform; p.49
pony; p.21
pool; p.52
popcorn; p.45
pork; p.11, 40
postcard; p.51
potato crisps; p.45
pub; p.8
pumpkin; p.24
rabbit; p.17
rain; p.17
raincoat; p.17
restaurant; p.8
rice; p.41
river; p.48
roast meat; p.41
roller-coaster; p.36
room; p.15
rooster; p.35
salad; p.12
salt; p.7, 44
salty; p.39
sand; p.20
sandals; p.53
sandcastle; p.33
sausage; p.25, 40
scarf; p.47, 53
sea; p.20
seafood; p.41
seashell; p.46

seat; p.16
seat belt; p.16
seesaw; p.18
sheep; p.17
shellfish; p.11
shower; p.15
shrimp; p.11, 40
skiing; p.47
sleeping-bag; p.37
slice; p.29
slide; p.18
snack; p.6
snack bar; p.8
snorkel; p.46
snow; p.47
snowball; p.47
snowman; p.47
soft; p.39
soft drink; p.13
son; p.18
soup; p.12, 26, 41
sour; p.39
souvenir; p.34
spade; p.33
spaghetti; p.26
spicy; p.39
spinach; p.43
spoon; p.7, 22
square; p.50
squid; p.11, 40
stamp; p.51
starfish; p.46
station; p.30
steak; p.25, 41
stew; p.41
subway; p.30
sugar; p.44
sun; p.20, 33
sunburn; p.32
sunglasses; p.52
sunscreen; p.33
supermarket; p.8
sweet; p.39
sweets; p.45
swimsuit; p.19, 53
swing; p.18
table; p.22, 38
taxi; p.30
tea; p.13
tent; p.37
theatre; p.50
ticket; p.31, 36, 49
to cook; p.44
to cycle; p.52
to dive; p.32

to drink; p.6
to drive; p.16
to eat; p.6
to feed; p.35
to go sightseeing; p.34
to jump; p.19
to land; p.16
to laugh; p.19
to order; p.23, 38
to play; p.19
to queue; p.36
to read; p.51
to receive; p.51
to run; p.19
to send; p.51
to serve; p.23, 38
to ski; p.32
to suntan; p.32, 52
to surf; p.32
to sweat; p.52
to swim; p.52
to take off; p.16
to travel; p.14, 31
to write; p.51
toilet; p.15
tomato; p.10, 27
tour; p.30
tour guide; p.30, 34
tower; p.50
tractor; p.21
traffic jam; p.16
train; p.49
trunks; p.19, 53
turkey; p.25
turnip; p.24
umbrella; p.17
vacation; p.14
valley; p.48
vinegar; p.7, 44
waiter; p.23
waitress; p.23
walnut; p.10
water; p.13
waterfall; p.48
wave; p.20
wine; p.13
yogurt; p.9